True

Crime

The Horrific Crimes And Accounts Of Some Of The Worlds Worst Murderers, Butcherers And Serial Killers

Volume 3

and consistent, in that any liability, in terms of inattention or otherwise, by any usage or abuse of any policies, processes, or directions contained within is the solitary and utter responsibility of the recipient reader. Under no circumstances will any legal responsibility or blame be held against the publisher for any reparation, damages, or monetary loss due to the information herein, either directly or indirectly.

Brody Clayton

Cover image courtesy of Flickr – Connor Tarter - https://www.flickr.com/photos/connortarter/475423150 2/

Table of Contents

Like FREE books?

Would you like them delivered to you every week?

Do you like non-fiction books on a huge range of different topics?

We send out FREE e-books every week so we can share our books with the world!

We have FREE books every week on AMAZON that we send to our email list.

So if you want in, then visit the link at the end of this book to sign up and sit back and wait for new books to be sent straight to your inbox!

Introduction

I want to thank you and congratulate you for purchasing the book, *"True Crime: The Horrific Crimes And Accounts Of Some Of The Worlds Worst Murderers, Butcherers And Serial Killers"*.

In 1984, a woman in Texas was placed on death row - her sentence divided the state: on one side were her supporters, claiming that she shouldn't be put to death, while on the other corner were her detractors who stipulated "an eye for an eye".

Before the 1970s, a deadly Candy Man was roaming free in Houston, Texas, before the police knew it, he had already killed 28 teenage boys. Was it the police's fault for not knowing better?

In the year 1978, one man led more than 900 people to "commit" suicide-- he was successful, but he too, was a casualty. How did he manage it?

For 30 years, a man performed various crimes, but he remained at large. Not once did his childhood indicate that he would grow up to be a murderer, but he did. What went wrong?

Lastly, a Bogeyman killed his family in their own home, but he was able to make a new life for himself. What drove him to do his filial crimes?

These are the cases we will be covering in this book... if you're ready for the unbelievable, proceed...

Thanks again, I hope you enjoy it!

Chapter 1:

The Texan's 14 Year Battle

Karla Faye Tucker could have fooled you: when she was not under the influence of countless illegal drugs, you could see her as her mother's perfect school girl, but beneath that exterior was a very troubled child, whose lamentations weren't heard, and so, it manifested through the worst possible violence: murder. Who was this murderess and why did her execution bring so much controversy to the state of Texas?

The Birthday Bash

A native of Houston, Texas, Karla Faye Tucker, born on November 18, 1959, was the youngest of three siblings. Not surprisingly, her parents lived a turbulent married life which brought Karla (and her sisters) some chaotic formative years.

At the age of 8, Karla had learned how to smoke, at the age of 10, her parents underwent a nasty divorce during which Karla learned that she was a product of an illegitimate affair. At 12, when she was only supposed to be thinking about homework and school projects, she had already experienced sex and drugs, and by the age of 14, she had already dropped out of school.

Right out of the classroom, she followed her mother Carolyn into prostitution; they also travelled with several boy bands until she reached the age of 16 when she married a mechanic named Stephen Griffith. In her twenties, Karla Faye brushed elbows with bikers, and in the process, met a woman named Shawn Dean, wife of Jerry Lynn Dean.

Later on, this couple introduced Karla to Danny Garrett-- the man who would help Karla commit what was to become known as the pickaxe murders. Danny and Karla became good friends (although it was Shawn who became Karla's best friend), but the world they lived in was filled with illegal drugs, sex orgies, and happy hours; on top of that, it also had a streak of psychological distortion.

Known as the "pill doctor" (someone who gives drugs to those who want it) Danny was famous for holding extreme parties where attendees were provided with almost unlimited booze, food, and drugs. On one particular weekend, the "pill doctor" decided to throw a birthday bash for Kari Ann, Karla's older sister.

The party went on and on for three days, where, as

expected, drugs such as Valium, Placidyl, Mandrex, and Dilaudid, were washed down by tequila, beer, or whisky. Soon enough, the attendees no longer had any form of inhibitions, nor were they thinking straight: the birthday girl wished to have sex orgies and everyone was eager to comply despite the dangers of sexually transmitted infections.

During this crazy drug fuelled bash, the dominant topic was the recent separation of married couple, Shawn and Jerry Dean. Apparently, about a week ago, Shawn left Jerry because of his physical abusiveness towards her - in fact, when Shawn attended Kari Ann's party, she was still sporting a busted nose and lip, courtesy of her husband.

No one knew that it was going to be Jerry's last assault on Shawn. And in fact it should have been the inspiration for Karla Faye and Danny Garrett to begin their ruthless murdering career.

Since Karla considered the abused woman as her best friend, she was extremely protective of her. In one later interview she said that she saw what "he did to her" and it made her feel the need to "get even with him, toe to toe, fist to fist".

As the party continued, Karla, Danny, Shawn, and another friend of theirs, Jimmy, huddled in the kitchen discussing how they felt about the wife-beating, Jerry Dean. While most participants of the get-together were busy with drugs and sex, the four were consumed with the idea of revenge, but nothing extreme-- only "kicking some ass" and doing something that "he will never forget".

One could say that their line of thought was only brought about by the drugs and booze they took, but later on, it would progress to a deep sense of animosity; one that would result in murder.

In the end, when Kari Ann and her friend, Ronnie, entered the kitchen, the hatred turned into laughter and light-hearted jokes until the thought of avenging Shawn died down to nothing but an idea. For Danny, the party had to end early because he still needed to attend his job as a bar tender in a local gin mill.

He needed a few hours to sober up so that he would be able to at least perform his job, albeit only half-heartedly. In the evening of June 12, Sunday, Karla drove him to his place of work and promised to pick him up again at 2:00 am, the time when the club closed.

Some of the attendees who were also heading home witnessed Karla and Danny heading out, so they said their goodbyes and thanks for a fun-filled weekend while the others were still inside the house, half-naked or half-asleep.

Jerry and Karla

After driving Danny, Karla went back to the house to find Shawn in a depressed state. She was drunk, the bottle of tequila still on her lap, and she was mumbling to Ronnie about how she hated Jerry for what he had done, and yet at the same time, how she still loved him. In the end, she fell asleep-- her feelings torn for her husband.

At this moment, Karla's revulsion for the 27 year old Jerry Lynn Dean was reinforced; apparently, even months ago, she had already developed a loathing for her best friend's husband. One particular occasion that fuelled this feeling was during Karla Faye's first stay in the Quay Point District of Houston, Texas.

Back then, Shawn and Jerry lived with her, but only because Karla treated the first as a friend. One time, she came home to find Jerry's Harley Davidson parked in her living room, beside the television where it was giving fuel fumes and to top it off, the oil was dripping on her floor. When asked why he placed it there, Jerry said it was for safety's sake.

While it was true that Karla had no qualms about living in a disorganized manner, it was a different story if someone else was making the mess, so eventually, she asked the couple to move out. Reports suggested that Karla had words with her motorcycle nemesis, but for Shawn's sake, the trouble was subdued.

Since then, whenever Karla and Jerry met, it was as if a big match was brewing-- in Karla's words: "We fought to fight". It even came to a point where the mere presence of one was an insult to the other; for example, when Karla saw Jerry silently sitting by his car, out of nowhere she punched him in the eye "just for being there".

It was clear that Jerry and Karla's relationship was far from being repaired; Shawn continued to hang out with Karla despite her husband's rules and this contributed to their daily disputes.

On the other hand, Jerry took pleasure in always deriding Karla to Shawn. The level of hate was so extreme that Shawn confided to her girlfriend that once, she saw Jerry stabbing a picture of Karla with a butcher knife.

His Precious Harley

Karla went out together with Jimmy to pick up Danny from his work, as agreed, it was around 2:00 am in the morning of June 13, 1983, Monday. Jimmy and Karla, only slightly recovered from the drugs and liquor binging, were having a good drive. They laughed at the slightest things around Quay Point which they hadn't noticed before: the wind, the weather, even the sounds.

For a while they talked about swimming and being active, but they sure couldn't go naked around the block and not be arrested, so they remained in their seats-- until Karla had an idea.

It was brilliant, at least in Karla's mind: all they had to do was steal Jerry's Harley Davidson and they would feel like all their Christmases had come early: a) what better way to insult Jerry and avenge Shawn, than to take the biker's most beloved Harley? b) They would certainly satisfy their need to be "active", and c) they would have extra money.

Jimmy liked it too, so on the way home together with Danny, they started planning. The three decided that the perfect time to steal the bike was that night (morning as it was almost 3:00 am), while they were still high and their desire for vengeance was still fresh.

Karla should come of course, because what good would it be if she hadn't? And besides that, she knew Jerry's apartment well - she knew that the area was easy to break into and that the cops would not be there because they hated the place. She was also sure that by the time they arrived there, Jerry would be fast asleep, probably because he would have smoked a couple of joints, as what his habit.

Back at home, they related their plan to a half-asleep Shawn, who liked the idea. According to her "it would teach that bastard a lesson", so she wished her friends, Jimmy, Karla, and Danny, good luck, and then went back to sleep.

As a camouflage, the three soon-to-be robbers dressed in all black, and finally, for protection, Danny asked Jimmy to take his shotgun from under the sofa. In the car, Danny also took a .38 from the compartment and hid it in one of his boots.

Later in one her interviews, Karla insisted that they never planned to hurt anyone and that their weapons were solely for protection (the area was well known to criminals, that's why police hated it).

The Pickaxe Murders

Once they reached their destination, they parked their car in a lot adjacent to Jerry's home and noticed that some of the street lights were lit. Danny was pissed off, to say the least, because if there were too many people roaming around, they wouldn't be able to steal the bike.

Nevertheless, they decided to continue and at least see how easy (or difficult) it would be to take the Harley. Asking Jimmy to stay outside to serve as the lookout, Karla and Danny went in and decided to break in, as they did so, the lights overhead flickered off -things were looking good for them.

Once they were in the front door, Danny grabbed the knob and twisted it, and surprisingly, it opened. The two couldn't believe their luck; not only was it already dark but they would just be entering, no breaking involved. Once inside, they were welcomed by the mixed smell of leather, metal, and fuel which could only mean one thing - the Harley was there, waiting for them.

Not wanting to rush things, they still remained motionless, waiting see whether anyone would come. When no one did, they turned the flashlight on and shone it around the room. It was a mess: garage tools were on the floor and several parts of the Harley were disassembled. Somewhere in the corner, there was a shovel and a pickaxe.

Karla was disappointed because she wanted to ruin a perfectly assembled bike, but she later reasoned that a stripped Harley was just as good-- after all, they would not be able to steal the whole motorcycle.

However, a booming voice from the bedroom yelled: "Who's out there?"

Apparently, Jerry's bedroom was near the "garage" and he had heard them moving around the room. He moved, creating a squeaking sound from the mattress before he flicked on his light. Later, Karla admitted that she was torn between escaping and fighting Jerry, but before her decision was made, Danny grabbed a hammer and went straight to the bedroom.

With nothing else to do, she followed Danny and saw him hit Jerry with the hammer-- right on his head. Blood splattered on the bed and Jerry was forced backward, unconscious, but it didn't stop Danny from hitting him some more.

Karla stood by and watched, and later on, she would report feeling extremely aroused by the whacking - so much so that the mere sight drove her to have multiple orgasms.

Her desire to participate in the magnetic act was stopped when she noticed that there was a woman beside Jerry, a woman who was poorly trying to conceal herself amidst the thick blanket and pillows. Unfortunately for her, Karla sighted her.

Seething with anger at the thought that while her friend, Shawn, was still at home, beaten and battered, but contemplating the fact that she still adored her husband, Jerry had already found a new tramp to bed.

Karla didn't waste any time; she went back to the garage and took the first weapon she saw - a three-foot long pickaxe - and then went back to the bedroom where Danny already had satiated his desired to flatten Jerry's skull.

Not thinking twice, Karla hurled the pickaxe at the woman and never stopped once, in fact, the more that the woman shook, the more Karla Faye hit her until her body turned into a bloody mush.

Danny watched his girl and had an idea: he took a blanket and instructed Karla to cover her eyes and then hit the target with the pickaxe, like a "piñata". After finishing the woman off, who would be later identified as Deborah Thornton, she delivered two more blows to Jerry Lynn Dean.

Perhaps they weren't thinking straight, or may be they wanted the world to know of their murders, but Danny and Karla left the pickaxe behind, tightly embedded in Deborah's heart.

The Controversial Execution

The murderers were not afraid to boast about what they had done - they never attempted to hide. For them, what they had done was just no big thing, nothing serious: just another wife-beating man and her tramp gone. No big deal.

It didn't take long for the police to put two and two together, especially when Karla and Danny's friends talked as soon as the police got rough. Everyone in the party confessed things, Shawn, Jimmy (who would later be acquitted as he didn't partake in the murder, his defence team insisted that he was a lookout for a burglary, not killing), and Kari Ann.

Before they knew it, Karla and Danny were in custody, and in September of the same year, the two were indicted for two counts of first-degree murder. They were tried separately, with Karla pleading "Not Guilty" as instructed by her lawyers. Unlike her, Danny Garrett wouldn't reach the end of his trial for he died of a liver disease while in prison.

Jury selection started on March 2, 1984, and ended on April 9. Testimony started on April 11 and was concluded on April 18. On the next day, April 19, the final arguments were heard, and the jury released a "Guilty" verdict to the murderess Karla Faye Tucker.

For 14 years, she would endure a waiting game: appeal after appeal would be made to free her from the death penalty - they would be sent to the state penal directors, to the Supreme Court, and eventually, to the then governor of Texas, George W. Bush.

All of them would reject her pleas. From Houston, she was transferred to Mountain View Prison in Gatesville, Texas as a death row convict. Release was probably impossible and Karla Faye knowing this, she told the reporters that if there was one thing she could have done differently, it would have been her plea of Not Guilty.

From her point of view, if she had pleaded otherwise, then the sentence couldn't have been execution as the state did not normally insist on giving out the death penalty to female convicts, on top of that, it was a wonder why she even denied the murders when it was so obvious that she was one of the killers.

Her defence team pointed out several flaws in the verdict, the first being the lack of evidence that the murders were premeditated. In Karla's case, she maintained from Day 1 that there was no intent-- it was a "spur of the moment decision".

Her lawyers argued that drugs (which she conceded on

taking the night of the murder), played a big role, and the the need to avenge her friend, Shawn. Some of her teammates also included her troubled childhood in her defence.

Year after year, Karla would find hope, only to lose it again. In the midst of the chaos, she found religion - she claimed that after her one of the trials, she was holding a Bible in her cell and was reading it, confused about what it all meant, and then all of a sudden, she was kneeling and asking God to forgive her.

Even her doubters related that her values and attitudes really changed for the better. In fact, Karla found love in the person of Dana Brown, her prison Minister. The two married in a Christian wedding right inside the prison.

Even Deborah's brother, Ron Carlson, who once detested Karla for what she had done, found it in his heart to forgive. He confided that initially, he felt not just anger - he also felt the need to kill Karla; he wanted to be on the other side, the one holding the pickaxe, and her (Karla) the one at his mercy.

He insisted that his poor sister was just at the wrong place, at the wrong time, but Karla and Danny didn't hesitate to take her life - brutally, like a piece of meat. "It made me sick," he once said during an interview.

But Carlson, like the woman he hated the most, found religion, and although the road to forgiveness wasn't easy, he was able to cross it. He told the reporters that he knew the anger was consuming him, so something had to be done, and that was to forgive Karla Faye.

So one day, he went to Mountain View, asking to visit the controversial woman on death row. Karla, according to Carlson, cried and apologised for what she had done, and he accepted it.

Since then, the two became friends and Carlson became a regular visitor. Soon enough Ron Carlson became one of Karla's most avid supporters who wanted her to be removed from death row. After 14 years of battle, however, Karla Fay Tucker's chances of remaining alive dove to zero.

On February 3, 1998, Governor George W. Bush released a statement saying that his office had truly received countless letters supporting the "changed" Texan murderess; most of those pleas were asking that Bush would accept their request to delay Karla's execution for another month.

But the Governor insisted that Karla Faye Tucker was guilty, and that the Supreme Court of the United States had already reviewed the case as best as they possibly could, so despite his respect for her supporters, he couldn't grant the delay.

From Mountain View, Karla was transferred to Huntsville State Prison where the execution (lethal injection) chamber was; there she had her last meal together with her husband, Dana Brown, some of her family members, and Ron Carlson, her victim's forgiving brother.

A writer at the scene asked Karla what she would be thinking once she was in the chamber, and she replied: "I'm certainly going to be thinking about what it's like in heaven."

Her last statement still included an apology for Jerry Lynn Dean's and Deborah Thornton's family: "I'm so sorry, I hope God will give you peace with this."

In her last moments, the attendants said she coughed twice, before silently reciting a prayer, and waited for the drugs to take effect.

Karla Faye Tucker was no more.

Chapter 2:

The Candy Man's Murderous Desires

"Dean Corll" by US Military - US Military. Licensed under Public Domain via Wikimedia Commons - https://commons.wikimedia.org/wiki/File:Dean_Corll.jpg#/media/File:Dean_Corll.jpg

A frantic phone call, made by a boy, alerted the Pasadena police, to a murder in the early hours of August 8, 1973. When the police arrived at 2020 Lamar Drive, Elmer Wayne Henley, Timothy Cordell Kerley, and Elmer's girlfriend, Rhonda Williams, were waiting so they could explain the horrors they had experienced the night before.

According to their story, Elmer (17) invited his 19 year old friend, Timothy, to join him at a party at Dean Corll's house. The party consisted of sniffing paint fumes and glue, as well as drinking alcohol. After partying for a few hours, the two friends left Dean Corll's house to buy sandwiches before taking a drive by Rhonda's home.

At that time, Rhonda was experiencing problems with her family and was in the act of running away after her father beat her abusively. Elmer, not knowing the dangers it could cause, offered a safe shelter in Corll's house and invited Rhonda to the party as well.

Dean was famous around the neighborhood for his drug and alcohol infused parties that he often hosted for young, teenage boys. But when the boys (Elmer and Timothy) came back with a girl (Rhonda), the serial killer got a little angry, although at that time, it didn't manifest into anything harmful.

After sniffing paint and drinking alcohol, the youths fell unconscious for a few hours. By the time one of them, Elmer, woke up, it was too late for escape: Dean Corll had them in handcuffs and had duct taped Rhonda's and Timothy's mouths.

Timothy was lying naked on the floor, while Rhonda still had her clothes on. The murderer told Elmer that he was very mad because he had brought his girlfriend to his house, all the while telling him that he was going to kill all three of them, but not before he tortured and assaulted Timothy first.

He dragged Elmer into the kitchen and pressed a .22 caliber pistol to his stomach. The teenager tried to calm Dean down by offering to help in the torture and murder of his friends - surprisingly, Dean agreed, so he released Elmer.

By cooperating, Dean meant that they (him and Elmer) had to engage in sexual games with the other two victims before killing them. They dragged Rhonda and Timothy into the bedroom, where they tied them to Dean's torture board. Rhonda was tied on her back, while Timothy was tied on his stomach.

When Rhonda and Timothy woke up, the game had already started; she asked Elmer if what was happening was real, to which he answered "Yes". Elmer asked if he could take Rhonda to another room, but Dean only ignored him.

Thinking that Dean's mind was somewhere else, he took the gun and pointed it at the serial killer however Dean Corll didn't falter.

In fact, it made him even madder and he started chasing after the boy, yelling "Kill me Wayne! You won't do it!" Soon after, Elmer got mad and shot him with the same gun Dean threatened him with in the kitchen.

When asked by the police, Elmer Wayne Henley stated he shot Dean Corll because he wanted to save himself and his friends, but soon, the police would find out the entire story behind the self-defense murder.

The detective found Dean Corll's body lying naked on the floor with 6 bullet holes in his back and shoulder. The sight in the bedroom was even more horrifying. Sex toys and handcuffs were lying around the room, leading the detectives to believe that this shooting was not an ordinary homicide.

The police continued searching Corll's house for evidence, and in every room they found a little piece of information that ultimately led them to the whole truth. Other than the handcuffs used for the latest victims, 8 other pairs were found around the entire residence.

They also found petroleum jelly, plastic wraps, ropes, and binding tapes. In the garage, the police found Corll's van, where a small wooden coffin-like box was waiting for a new young body. When they discovered the whole story, the state of Texas was shocked and repulsed.

Confessions from the Accomplice

Corll was well liked in the neighborhood and everyone thought he was a nice person. A good looking, friendly man, always happy to lend a helping hand, no one in the neighborhood was afraid to leave their teenager in his company. But it was only a facade.

Many teenagers were known to hang out at his parties not because it was innocently fun-filled, but because they had easy access to drugs and alcohol. He often took the neighborhood kids in his van, driving them to or from the school for several years before the murderer's true face was revealed.

Elmer Wayne Henley was one of those boys who enjoyed spending time with Dean Corll. It wasn't surprising; the man was interesting to the young boys because he showed them how to have fun, and often threw a blasting party.

Elmer told the police that one of the reasons he killed Dean was because he had a warehouse full of dead bodies. The police officers were skeptical of this accusation even after Elmer started giving out names.

The frightened teenager not only gave the names of three missing young boys, but shared the possible location where many bodies could have been buried.

Elmer then took them to a boat storage facility in Houston

where Dean had rented a shed. The floor of the shed was only half covered with carpet; the rest was bare and covered with junk and a few shovels. The ground seemed freshly dug.

The young teenager was as pale as a ghost upon seeing the sight, so the detectives started to believe his story. The Police then dug up the floor of the shed, under which they found a layer of white lime, which had also been found in Dean's home.

Underneath that layer, just 6 inches below the ground, the police dug out their first victim. A few hours later, a second, more decomposed body was discovered, also belonging to a young teenager. By the end of the day, the police had organized a systematic dig in Dean's shed to uncover the bodies faster.

By midnight, 8 bodies had been dug out of the shed and sent to a medical examiner for identification and autopsy. The police took a child's bike and clothes from the shed as evidence and talked to the warehouse manager. They discovered that Dean Corll had rented the shed 2 years ago, came in twice or thrice a week, and had even wanted to rent a second shed.

The detectives took Henley back to their headquarters for further questioning. The more he talked, the more the detectives realized he may not be the hero who saved Pasadena from a serial rapist and a murderer. He was also an accomplice.

The Other Accomplice

By the time Elmer had revealed the names of the victims and the location where their bodies were hidden, another witness had come forward to the police, blowing the case wide open. His name was David Brooks and he confessed to helping Dean find his victims.

When the detectives told Elmer that his friend, David, had confessed to assisting Dean, the teenager seemed relieved and said that he could finally tell the whole story now.

Elmer Henley and Dean Corll's relationship started when Elmer was about 14 years old. Elmer looked up to him, as Dean was an older man who could teach him a thing or two. David Brooks, however, was even closer to Dean. He was one of Dean's many teenage friends.

He even accompanied him to Texas' beaches, rode his motorbike, and socialized with other young boys. When David's mother and father divorced, he dropped out of high school and soon, left Houston to live with his mother. Each time he came to visit his father though, he was known to stay at Dean's house for a few days.

A sexual relationship soon developed between the two, when the older man offered to pay David to perform fellatio. The teenager wasn't traumatized by this, in fact, he considered Dean's place his second home.

David admitted to the police that he and Elmer often lured young boys, sometimes their friends, other times young people they met in the Heights, and took them to Corll's home for a party. David stated he never had anything to do with the torture or killing, but implied that Elmer knew a little more.

And it was true; Elmer was deeply involved in the violent game. According to reports, while he and his friends (Timothy and Rhonda) were waiting for the police to arrive in front of Dean's porch, David told Timothy that he could've gotten 200 dollars for bringing him in.

Throughout the questioning, he told of other locations where Dean had buried his victims. Other than the boat shed, bodies of young men were also found at the High Island Beach and Lake Sam Rayburn. The two accomplices escorted the police during the search, and showed them the exact locations where young bodies had been buried.

The complete victim list turned out to be at least 28 men, between the ages of 13 and 20, most of them in their mid-teenage years. The pedophile tied them to his torture board and molested them for hours, sometimes even days. He sometimes ordered them to write to their parents to let them know they are "alright".

In several cases, two boys were assaulted at the same time. After the pervert had his fun with his victims, he would then kill them either with the gun found in his home or by strangulation. His two accomplices were paid 200 dollars for each victim lured into Dean's home.

The sweet deal lasted for 3 years, from 1970 to 1973. Although they did not confess to killing or torturing anyone, the police believed they had been involved in the murder and cover up of 6 teenagers. They were both convicted to life in prison with little chance of parole.

How the Rapist Came To Be

Dean Corll was known as a quiet and shy kid, but people around him knew how he cared for others' well being. His parents divorced several years after his younger brother was born, and both tried to reconcile for the sake of their children soon after, but their reunion didn't last long.

His father showed very little affection toward the young boys and sometimes, he was even harsh. Dean suffered from rheumatic fever, which went unnoticed and resulted in a heart condition. His mother remarried and the family opened a small candy company that sold most of their products in Houston, Texas.

They lived in Vidor, where Dean finished high school as a loner, although he was known to date a couple of girls during his teenage years. He and his brother worked in the candy company, which in time, meant the family relocated to Houston.

His mother asked him to move in with his widowed grandmother in Indiana. There, he had a relationship with a girl, but refused her marriage proposal and moved back to Houston to help out with the company.

When his mother divorced her second husband, she opened a new candy company, where Dean was made vice president. A teenage employee complained that Dean had made inappropriate advances to him, but his overprotective mother fired the teenager instead of punishing her son.

Some believe Dean discovered his homosexual tendencies during his service in the US Army. Acquaintances later revealed that it was only after his service in the army that he changed his attitude toward teenage boys. After he ended his military service, his family's candy company moved its headquarters to the street across from an elementary school.

Dean became known there as the Candy Man, because he always gave out free candy and even installed a pool table where the children were welcome to gather and have fun. Later, acquaintances would say he was always flirtatious towards teenage boys.

It was there he met David Brooks when he was only 12 years old, and made friends with Elmer Henley when he was 14.

The Police Investigation

Houston, Texas was an industrial city at the beginning of the 70's, with several areas of the city booming, while others were experiencing economic decline. One of these areas where the social and economic status was declining was the district known as The Heights.

Many young, teenage boys were reported missing, but the police dismissed them as voluntary runaways. By the time the Corll Case was reported, around 50 teenage boys were already reported missing – all only from The Heights. The police department responsible for Corll's case was criticized for their lack of effort, dedication, and time.

For even when Elmer and David had confessed some of

the burial grounds, they were still reluctant to investigate. For instance, the search was abandoned on August 13, in spite of Elmer's claims that there were two more bodies buried on the beach.

The workers in his candy company said he was seen digging in parts of the business and acting strangely long before 1970. The first time he was caught by employees, he said that he was just burying spoiled candies which could caused an insect infestation.

He soon cemented the area, and the claim was never investigated by the police. Later, he was seen digging in a waste ground, which was soon transformed into a car park where a search for victims became very difficult.

The police once again stopped the search even though a skull, pelvis, and another bones were found. When the skull was used in a reconstruction by forensic specialists, it was determined that it belonged to a missing teenage boy from Houston.

The two accomplices insisted that Dean was involved in an organization that provided services for perverts like him, but they were not believed. In 1975, the police found pornographic photos and films, in which 11 of Corll's identified victims were recognized.

The search led to the arrest of five people in Dallas and

California, but Dean was not linked with their pedophile organization at the time. The authorities believed that since neither David nor Elmer mentioned other pedophiles, films, or photos, the allegations were not true.

With further forensic development in the years following 2008, several other victims were found and the police today can link them with the serial killer from Houston. No one can say why the police did not investigate the case further-- perhaps it was because the killer had long since died?

Some were relieved to hear the case is closed, others were happy to put these gruesome crimes behind them. One thing's for sure: no one trusted a strange Candy Man after this spree of torture and murder.

Chapter 3:

One Leader, Nine Hundred Deaths

"02-jones-jim ji" by Jonestown Institute. Licensed under Attribution via Wikimedia Commons - https://commons.wikimedia.org/wiki/File:02-jones-jim_ji.jpg#/media/File:02-jones-jim_ji.jpg

They say evil is not born – it is created. In the case of

James Warren Jones, the evil must have been created right after his birth. Born in the midst of the Great Depression, his parents lost their family farm, while his father was left disabled in a gas accident during WWI.

He grew up in the small and racially divided town of Lynn, Indiana, where poverty was all around him. Being a WWI veteran who couldn't provide for his family was difficult for his father to accept so his father began drinking to drown out his perceived failure.

According to Jones' schoolmates and family members, it caused a great deal of pain and shame to Jones that he was one of the poorest boys in his town. He sympathized with the African American community because of their low social status, even though he claimed his father was a member of the KKK (Ku Klux Klan).

It was noted that his father told him not to bring home African Americans, after the one time he came back from school with a black schoolmate. Unlike the neglect and latent aversion he received from his father, his mother pushed him to be ambitious and to search for the American Dream.

She was the head of the house, having to work various jobs to support the family, and even though she was educated and ambitious, she couldn't get ahead because she lived in a period of gender discrimination in America, when women were not accustomed to take on a leading role in society.

In the book Tim Reiterman wrote about Jones, he stated that his mother always taught him to make something of himself, so he won't become like his father.

Even as an only child, Jones still spent very little time with his parents. His neighbors and school friends reported that as a toddler, he would often be seen unattended and covered in filth. In their home, dessert was never served, and the family never dined together.

There was no affectionate display of emotions and the family kept a distance between each other. According to recent evaluations, this type of neglect, social mutilation, and emotional scarring give way to megalomaniac and narcissistic personality developments. Perhaps it was true even in Jim's time.

His school records showed a smart pupil, who was not fond of physical activity, but enjoyed reading and giving speeches to his classmates. Jones attended many church ceremonies in Lynn and visited every church in the town. He even held religious readings or school lectures in his backyard.

In middle school, he could be seen dressed in a white

sheet, sharing religious wisdom to sinners of Lynn. Although most of his classmates took him as a weirdo and he was often socially excluded, in the backyard of his house, he was in total control and anxiety free.

He would hold lectures for hours, not allowing his friends to leave; he even locked up several of his peers one day to see how they might react. On one occasion, his friend, Donald Foreman, tried to leave so Jones shot him with a gun.

His intelligence, oratory skills, and mental capacity helped him feel superior to his peers: a compensation for the neglect he received as a child and as a young adolescent, as well as for his low economic status.

He had been a reader since he was a child, and throughout his teenage and adolescent years, he was impressed by the works of Marx, Stalin, Zedong, Hitler, and Gandhi. His acquaintances remember him as a weird kid obsessed with religion and death. He held funerals for animals and may even have stabbed a cat to death.

When his parents divorced, he and his mother moved to Indiana, where the boy graduated with honors from Richmond High School. A year later, he married Marceline Baldwin and a few years after, they moved to Indianapolis. There, he earned a degree in secondary education by attending a night school.

Mixing Politics with Religion

Growing into a true socialist, Jones became frustrated with the excommunication of open communists in America at the time, so he thought of his own way of demonstrating Marxism. He was well received among several political organizations at first, especially by politicians like Willie Brown and Harvey Milk, and was even appointed director of the Human Rights Commission and chairman of the Housing Authority Commission in San Francisco.

He managed to integrate the police department, Telephone Company, an amusement park, theater, and many restaurants with the church, but was criticized and was asked to restrain his public actions regarding the African American communities.

After spending years in the search for the right church and not being able to fit into any mainstream religious organization, the then student pastor at the Somerset Methodist Church, branched out and formed the *Wings of Deliverance Church.*

Inspired by Father Divine, a religious leader since the 20's, and proclaiming himself as an evangelist and a healer, he gathered his first followers. The church then changed its name into the People's Temple.

His supporters believed that Jones was following in the footsteps of Father Divine, and all their donated money was going to a communal cause, when in fact, it ended up in Jones' pockets. Jones continued to win people over with his fiery rhetoric, healing sessions, and false high moral standing.

And while openly discouraging romantic relationships, sex, and even dancing, he was involved in many adulterous affairs, and had more than one illegitimate child. Slowly, but surely, he started preaching that he and his priesthood were more valuable than familial relationships.

He encouraged his supporters to call him Father, God, Savior, sometimes even Dad. He staged healing assemblies, where his nurses would choose a member of the audience and take them backstage, where they were healed and their tumor removed. The nurse would later parade the fake tumor around the attendees as proof of their Father's healing powers.

The American elite were not ready to accept equality between white people and other races just yet, so Jones was widely criticized and restricted. He and his wife became the first couple to adopt a black orphan in Indiana. They also had other adopted children from different races, mostly children left behind by the Korean War.

He preached that other people should help the scattered people from the war and adopt their refugee children. He and his "rainbow" family, as he called them, moved to Brazil, where he intended to open another church.

Afraid of being attacked as a white communist in a foreign country, he preached his ideas of a communal lifestyle, rather than Marxism, while exploring the various religions in Brazil. When his fellow preachers told him that his church was on the verge of collapse without his presence, he came back with his family.

In the 60's, he and a 100 of his followers moved to California. By the 70's the church had expanded to San Francisco. His sermons included speeches of him stating he was the incarnation of Jesus, Buddha, Gandhi and Lenin.

His wife was interviewed by the New York Times, where she stated that her husband was promoting Marxism with the help of religion. Jim Jones when speaking to John Maher called him an atheist and agnostic. He was seen stomping on the Bible, saying to his followers that the same black book had held them back for 2000 years.

Torture, Murders and Suicides in the Prison Camp

Eventually, in 1977, a tax evasion case fell on the Jones temple, so he and his 1000 or so most devoted followers moved to Guyana. He bought some land where he intended to create a self-sufficient agricultural utopia for his followers in the jungle.

He named it Jonestown. The members of his church who stayed behind and the relatives of those who moved to Jonestown told the police of the brutal beatings and suicidal manipulation the Reverend was conducting.

But having the support of many politicians in the US, offering free food and shelter for the poor and disabled, Jones was left alone and he continued his "mission". There, he spoke of being the only true heterosexual, but was seen sexually abusing a man during one speech, allegedly, to test the man's homosexual tendency.

In 1973 however, he was arrested and charged for soliciting sex from a man in a movie theater restroom in LA. In their communal utopia, Jones could not hide his drug addiction anymore, so he lost the respect of many inner circle members. He was apparently fond of hallucinogens and amphetamines.

But Jones was not the only one on drugs in his community. Detailed records were kept on each resident, where ample amounts of Valium, Demerol, Thorazine, sodium pentathol, and chloral hydrate were administered.

The American pathologist inspecting the site after the mass suicide said that there were enough drugs for a city with a population of 66,000. According to the cult, the drugs were given so they could control the members' behavior.

Their promised paradise did not turn out as expected. The people were stuck working all day, from 7 in the morning to 6 or 7 in the evening, for 6 days a week. In turn, they were given only beans and rice, while their leader feasted on meat, eggs, and soft drinks from a separate, private refrigerator.

As a result of malnutrition and psychological abuse, high fevers and severe diarrhea circulated throughout the commune. Psychological abuse and punishment were a custom in Jones, community.

Kids were not allowed to see their real parents during the day; they addressed Jones as Dad and were given a brief time during the night to be with their parents. If the children disobeyed, the favorite disciplinary punishment in the commune was to leave the child down a well overnight, sometimes tied upside down.

Jones had them believe that there was a monster living there, when in fact, his henchman were hiding, pulling the children by their legs. Other methods were used on older members, like standing in a small (6x4x3 foot) plywood box.

Often, if they tried to escape and got caught, they were drugged to the point of helplessness. Guards surrounded the commune day and night, making sure everyone stayed where they were.

His maniacal leadership reached its peak many times before the actual mass suicide. Residents who escaped the commune later testified that Jones tested their loyalty by instructing them to drink some type of red juice, which they were told was poison.

They were also told that they would die within 45 minutes, while the madman observed their reaction. All residents drank the juice and waited for their death, including children. When the poison proved to be juice after an hour, Jones told them they had proven their loyalty to him.

He also told them that the time when they were to end

their own lives was not so far away. Around $65,000 each month was appointed to Jones, all coming from the residents' welfare payments. His wealth was estimated to be over 26 million dollars.

Trouble in Paradise

The stories of the prison camp soon spread through the news. Former members of the cult started speaking out and Congressman Leo Ryan decided to visit the cult himself. On November 18, 1978, he gathered television and newspaper crews and planned a rescue operation.

The crowd walked around the commune, convincing them to leave with them. Some people decided to leave, and together with the congressman and media crew, they were driven to Port Kaituma. Just when they thought their plan had worked, gunmen sent by Jones started shooting.

They had infiltrated the rescue team under the pretense that they wanted to leave Jonestown too. Some defectors noticed on of the gunmen and recognising him as a loyal pet of Jones', tried to notify the congressman, however he was let onto the plane anyway. As soon as he got onto the plane, he started shooting and the other gunmen joined him, leaving 5 people dead.

Congressman Ryan, NBC newspaperman Don Harris,

NBC cameraman Bob Brown, Examiner photographer Greg Robinson and defector Patricia Parks all died on the spot. Of all the shooters, only Larry Layton, the infiltrator was accused of the shooting.

Congressman Leo Ryan

In the meantime, the mad preacher had decided on a final action. Valium and cyanide were mixed to create a toxic punch, which was distributed around the cult members. The guards instructed the people to drink the poison, and when some refused, they were held at gunpoint until they drink the poison.

276 children died first and the total victim count was 909 people. Jones was found lying lifeless on the camp's main pavilion, shot in the head and surrounded by his wife, nurse and inner circle cult members.

Brody Clayton

Pictures of those who died in Jonestown

"Jonestown Memorial Service Pictures" by Symphony999 - Own work. Licensed under CC BY-SA 3.0 via Wikimedia Commons

Chapter 4:

Robinson's Money and Murders

If you believe that everything was easier 50 years ago, remember that it was easier for criminals too. At least that was true in the case of John Edward Robinson. He was committing crimes for 30 years before he got caught.

Born in a suburb of Chicago, as the third of five children of Henry and Alberta Robinson, John's beginnings did not show many signs of violence. His father was an alcoholic and his mother was a disciplinarian, but the young Robinson seemed to be under control at the time.

He joined the Eagle Scouts and traveled to England, where they reportedly performed before Queen Elizabeth II. He registered at a private school for priests, but dropped out a year later because of disciplinary issues.

Robinson enrolled at his hometown Morton Junior College, wanting to become an X-ray technician, but dropped out of there too after two years. He moved to Kansas in 1964 and married his wife Nancy, with whom he had three children.

Perpetrator's First Crimes

Robinson's first crime was in Kansas in 1969, when he embezzled 33,000 dollars from Dr. Graham's medical practice, where he worked. He was caught forging the credentials he used to get the job and was sentenced to three years of probation. A year later, he violated his probation by moving to Chicago without the permission of his probation officer.

He got a job at the R.B. Jones Company as a salesman, from where he embezzled funds and got his probation extended. He was ordered to go back to Kansas, where his probation was extended yet again in 1975, this time for security and mail frauds.

Although already a criminal during his stay in Kansas, he tried to appear as a typical family man. Robinson became a baseball coach, Sunday school teacher, and a Scoutmaster, and he even managed to get himself on the board of directors of a local charitable organization.

But in the mind of the criminal, this normal lifestyle would not hold for very long. Soon, he forged letters from the executive director to the mayor and then from the mayor to municipal leaders, to acclaim his volunteer efforts for the community.

These forgeries got him selected as the Man of the Year in

the charitable organization, and he even received a celebratory lunch in his honor. His probation was finally completed in 1979, but only a year later, Robinson committed yet another crime.

He was sentenced to 60 days in jail for check forgery and embezzlement in 1982, but soon after his release he started with his felonies again. This time, Robinson convinced a friend to invest 26,000 dollars in a counterfeit hydroponics business and promised a quick turnaround, so his friend could pay for his dying wife's medical bills.

During this time, Robinson started to make sexual advances to his neighbors' wives which provoked a fistfight with one of his neighbors. He also later stated, it was at this point, that he became a member of a sadomasochism cult, where victims were lured in, tortured, and raped.

He was claiming that he had become the Slavemaster of a cult he named International Council of Masters. Later, many people believed he used the women in BDSM activities with clients, although these allegations were never proven.

From Frauds to Murders

The first woman to disappear after being associated with Robinson was a 19 year old woman named Paula Godrey. He offered her job training and employment in one of his fraudulent companies. When she moved to work for Robinson, she disappeared and was never seen again.

After not hearing from her for several days, her family reported her missing. The police questioned Robinson, but he stated that he had no knowledge of her whereabouts. A few days later, her family received a letter with her signature at the bottom, saying that she was okay, but did not want to see them again.

The police terminated the investigation because there was no evidence to suggest any wrongdoing and Paula was an adult. A few months later, Robinson met Lisa Stasi under the name John Osborne and on the pretense of being a Good Samaritan.

He promised her a job, daycare for her 4 month daughter, and an apartment in Chicago, but like Paula, Lisa was never seen again. Her daughter, Tiffany, however, was taken by Robinson and was sold to his brother and his wife, a couple who hadn't had any success in adopting.

Apparently, when Robinson approached Lisa, he asked her to sign a couple of blank sheets of paper and he used those signatures for the legal adoption papers. Years later, the couple revealed that Robinson told them that the mother of the child took her own life.

Robinson's third victim was 27 year old Catherine Clampitt. She moved to Kansas City to look for a job and landed right in the lap of the predator. Robinson promised her a new wardrobe and extensive travel, but she too vanished the same year.

During his prison sentence, he met the prison librarian Beverly Bonner. She left her husband to move to Kansas to work for Robinson. After some time, he convinced her to forward her alimony checks to a Kansas post office, and her family never saw her again. Robinson, however, received her alimony checks for several years after her disappearance.

In the 90's Robinson took advantage of the Internet and started searching for his prey on social networking sites. His first victim was the 45 year old Sheila Faith and her 15 year old daughter Debbie. He posed as a wealthy man who could give Sheila a job, support her and her daughter, and pay for Debbie's therapy, who was wheelchair-bound. Once they moved to Kansas, they disappeared, but Robinson continued cashing her pension checks for the next 7 years.

On social networking sites, Robinson appeared under the name Slavemaster and became popular in BDSM chat rooms. He offered a job in Kansas to a 21 year old Izabela Lewicka, a Polish settler living in Indiana. She moved to Kansas in 1999 and agreed to a bondage relationship.

Robinson even gave her an engagement ring, took her to the county registrar, and paid for a marriage license, but never came back to pick it up. They were seen many times in public, where they often told people different stories of how they had known each other.

Before she disappeared, she signed a lengthy slave contract with 115 items, which gave Robinson control over her bank accounts and every aspect of her life. During the time Robinson "took care" of Lewicka, he encouraged another woman, Suzette Trouten to move to Kansas. She was to be his submissive sex slave and they were going to travel the world together.

Suzette was a lonely nurse from Michigan, who had been in a BDSM relationship for 11 years, so she agreed. Her mother reported that she received several letters from her daughter, where she stated that she was abroad with Robinson, but the postmarks on the envelopes were always from Kansas City and the letters were mistake-free, which was unusual.

After so many years of spreading terror, the predator finally became reckless and did not cover his tracks well. His name started coming up in many missing person reports, so authorities from both Missouri and Kansas focused on looking at him a little deeper.

In 2000, a woman filed a complaint against him and he was charged with stealing sex toys. With the theft charges, the police could finally obtain a search warrant and catch this predator.

He was arrested on his farm near La Cygne in Kansas. On the farm, the police found the bodies of only two of his victims, Suzette Trouten and Izabela Lewicka. Their bodies were placed in 85 pound barrels.

The Police searched the garages Robinson rented in a storage facility and found three similar barrels with three corpses inside. They were identified as Sheila Faith, Debbie Faith and Beverly Bonner. All victims were killed in the same way, with one or more blows to the head with a blunt instrument, probably a hammer.

Sentencing the Villain

In 2002, Robinson faced trial. He was held accountable in the state of Kansas for the deaths of Isabella Lewicka, Suzette Trouten, and Lisa Stasi and multiple other charges. He received life imprisonment for Stasi's murder and the death penalty for Lewicka and Trouten.

For interfering with parental custody, he was sentenced to 5 to 20 years in prison, 20 and a half years for the kidnapping of Trouten, and another 7 months for theft. His lawyers tried to avoid a trial in Missouri because the laws there were far less lenient than in Kansas.

Robinson did not want to cooperate with the authorities to help them find the bodies of his other victims, so a compromise was reached in October 2003. In the scripted plea, he was convicted for murdering the Faiths, Clampitt, Godfrey and Bonner and received a life sentence without parole for each case.

Today, at the age of 71, Robinson is still on death row, waiting to be the first prisoner executed by lethal injection in the state of Kansas.

The Aftermath

Most interestingly, Robertson's wife did not file for a divorce until 2005, after 41 years of marriage. She cited irreconcilable differences and incompatibility.

His brother's adopted daughter, which turned out to be Lisa Stasi's daughter, filed a suit against Karen Gaddis, a social worker at Truman Medical Center, for introducing Stasi to Robinson in 1984 without investigating his charitable organization that allegedly supported white unwed mothers with babies.

She won two rulings: the first one when the hospital agreed to pay an undisclosed sum, which she split with her biological grandmother, and another, when she managed to prevent Robinson from profiting from any future movie rights and book sales about the cases.

Another body stuffed in a chemical barrel was found in 2007, in a rural part of Iowa, where Robinson had an alleged business partner. The investigators said that the body was too decomposed to be identified and it would be hard to track down any possible victims, since Robinson was not cooperating.

According to them, there are probably many other barrels to be found, and bodies to be discovered.

Chapter 5:

18 Years in Hiding

John Emil List (1925-2008), also known as 'The Bogeyman of Westfield', was a mass murderer famous for the killing of his five-member family and successfully evading justice for eighteen years. A native of Bay City, Michigan, List was born into a German Lutheran family where religion was a major presence in his life.

His devout upbringing followed him well into adulthood, with the local pastor, Rev. Eugene Rehwinkel of Redeemer Lutheran Church, testifying that "He was always at church ... very predictable. I could tell you the pew he'd be sitting in."

In the mid-1960s, List had moved to Westfield from Rochester, N.Y. He exuded success, earning $25,000 a year as the vice president and controller of a local bank. With his money, he bought one of the fanciest houses in town.

The residents of this affluent suburb found the List family likable enough, but remembered John List as a profoundly aloof man. In fact, when a neighbor tried to approach them while bearing gifts (a pie), John List opened the door and said: "We don't socialize."

Things seemingly turned sour for John List following the 1970s. "Everything I tried seemed to fall to pieces", was his cry to his pastor in a rambling 5-page letter found at the scene of the crime.

Little did Westfield's suburbanites know that behind the carefully cultivated facade of money, was a man wrung by an $11,000 mortgage taken out on his mother's town home – he was also skimming from her financial accounts.

The unassuming accountant seemed an unlikely candidate for murder but severe financial debts coupled with the loss of his job and a less-than-happy family life may have contributed greatly towards the events that occurred that fateful day in November of 1971.

"I wasn't earning near enough to support us," he wrote to his pastor as a form of explanation.

Saving Their Souls

While the Westfield murders were performed on the spur of moment, the method of execution and details of escape had been plotted meticulously beforehand. By his own account, John had originally selected November 1, All Saint's Day, as "an appropriate day for them to get to heaven" but his travel plans forced him to delay until November 9.

That early fall morning in 1971, John shot his wife, Helen, in the back of the head with his 1912 Steyr 9 mm automatic, followed by the shooting of his mother, Alma, who stayed on the third floor of his Westfield mansion.

John's mother's killing seemed very unlikely since he was a devout son who had been extensively helped by his mother during his financial troubles, but he reasoned that it was an act of benevolence: because of his mother's old age, his crime would come as a shock, and he didn't want her to suffer because of him.

After this, it was speculated that he visited the bank to redeem some savings bonds. He then lay in wait for several hours for his children to return from school, who were surprised with bullets to their heads.

Perhaps the only detail that did not go according to plan was the unexpected return of his middle son, John Jr., from soccer practice. Nonetheless, the boy was found shot 10 times in the head and chest, unlike the other family members who were only shot once.

His self-confessed (and only) deviation from schedule at

the time was reading out prayers for his recently deceased family from a hymn book. His cold decision to carry on with the murders despite the time lapse between the first two and later three killings was explained by John in the following words – "After making the decision, there was no turning back. It's just like D-Day, you go in, there's no stopping after you start."

Following the crime, John Emil List cleaned the murder scene of blood and emptied the bullet casings into the trash can. The bodies (except for the 85-year old Alma's) were dragged upstairs and laid in body-bags in the classic ballroom.

On the dining table, he left out books and photos borrowed from his neighbor, Wittke, from whom the Westfield mansion had originally been purchased. His consideration extended so far as to attach a thank you note to the books, an apology letter to a few of his relatives, and a five-page letter of explanation to his pastor.

He then had dinner and went to sleep. The next morning, after turning all the lights on, in a determined attempt at absolution, John left the house with the radio blaring through the audio system, tuned in to a religious station.

Later, at the Connie Chung interview, when asked why he

did not attempt suicide, he answered "It was my belief that if you kill yourself, you won't go to heaven," he said. "I got to the point where I felt that I could kill them. Hopefully they would go to heaven, and I would have a chance to confess my sins to God and get forgiveness."

His Plotting and The Murder House

To this day, the highlight of the Westfield murders remains this: how five members of the List family went undiscovered for almost a month, and the perpetrator missing for eighteen years. John List's detailed escape plan had been spectacular, one could admit.

All daily deliveries to the Westfield List mansion were stopped and the children's institutions notified of a family emergency which would leave them unable to attend school. John's 16-year-old daughter, Patricia List, had informed her school coach of her father's worrying behavior and his threats to murder the children.

Despite driving by the house on the day of the murders, the coach was unaware of the horrors happening within, as the house was lit up and no disturbance was noted. It was only at the end of the month, when the lights began burning out, that the seemingly uninhabited house was reported to local law enforcement.

"It was so methodical, so cold-blooded," James Moran, Westfield's retired police chief remembered. "His mother and his wife were still in their bedclothes. He had even turned the thermostat down to 50 degrees to preserve the bodies."

In the year following the discovery of the murders in December 1971, the Westfield mansion was catapulted to a macabre sort of fame with people from miles around coming to stare at the house they had dubbed as the "Murder House". The house was subject to frequent break-ins by local children.

As a result, a few years after the murders, the Westfield mansion – the site of such blatant violence - was burnt down by intruder activity. Perhaps fittingly, the infamous ballroom went up in an inferno of flames. The perpetrators of the arson were never found or prosecuted.

"John's Been Caught"

Despite his meticulous planning and evasive maneuvers, John Emil List ended up living out the last of his days in prison. On May 1, 1990, jurors deliberated less than nine hours before convicting John Emil List, then 64, to five life terms served consecutively.

His arrest was deemed as 'unbelievable', coming hot on

the heels of tips called in by viewers of a FOX's 'America's Most Wanted' episode which showed an age-progressed bust of John Emil List.

What happened before his arrest?

Surprisingly, by 1977 (6 years after he murdered his family), John had reverted back to his former pattern of life under the alias of Robert Clark. To his new neighbors in Virginia, he was a devout churchgoing accountant, free of problems with the law.

Flipping through his tenant file, Carole Burton, manager of the east Denver apartment complex where John had stayed for eight years said, "The man did absolutely nothing to call attention to himself... there are no complaints in his file, no notices, no record of repairs, no nothing."

In 1977, at a church social, he met Delores Miller, whom he married in 1985. One friend, unidentified by the *New Leader* newspaper, said that John had told her that he had been married before to an alcoholic who died of cancer - "He told her she went through a slow, agonizing death."

11 days after John List's case was broadcast on America's Most Wanted, on 1st June 1989, 'The Bogeyman' was finally cornered, thanks to one of "Robert's" neighbors

who identified him as looking like *the* John E. List.

After his arrest, Robert Clark denied being John Emil List; however, the FBI was able to confirm his identity through fingerprints obtained at the crime scene from 18 years ago. When faced with irrefutable evidence, John confessed to being the perpetrator of the 18 year old killings.

However, his first public statement on the murders was free of remorse and worded in self-effacement. He said, "I wish to inform the court I remain truly sorry for the tragic events of 1971. I feel that because of my mental state at the time, I was unaccountable for what happened. I ask all affected by this for their forgiveness, understanding and prayer."

A court psychiatrist testified that he was suffering from obsessive compulsive disorder which resulted in the trail of destruction he left in his wake. But the judge remained unmoved.

Once Robert Clark had disintegrated, Dolores Miller disappeared from the public eye; she didn't attempt to visit John during the trial or after. Her reaction on the initial discovery of the murderer was "aghast": "This is not the man I know. The man I know is kind, loving, a devoted husband and a dear friend. He is a quiet man who loves his work and the people he works with."

Dolores was last reported to be living in poverty as of 2006. Public speculation still persists on whether she would have been John's sixth victim had he not been discovered. By her own account to neighbors, her husband was relapsing back into his earlier triggers for violence – the inability to keep up a steady job and a tendency to live beyond his means.

The relationship was strained at the time when Robert Clark was picked up by the FBI on suspicions of being John Emil List. After being placed in custody, two notes arrived in the Westfield cemetery, next to the List family's headstone.

The first said: "John's been caught. June 1, 1989," the other read: "Now you can rest in peace."

On March 21, 2008, List died in his Trenton, New Jersey, prison cell at the age of 82.

The Boy Scout's Tale

Since the capture and trial of John Emil List, the reasoning behind such atrocities had been a matter of public speculation. During the trials, his Defence put forward several accounts of the List's deteriorating family life. Dr. Henry Liss, a neurologist, testified that Helen List drank four or five glasses of Scotch a day, and was addicted to tranquilizers.

She was a sickly woman suffering from syphilis contracted from her first husband, a Korean War hero who had died overseas before she married List in 1951. Later, the disease progressed to cerebral palsy, leaving her a semi-invalid and blind in one eye. Ethically, morally and religiously, the venereal disease was unacceptable to List and added to his distaste of his family's affairs.

To John Emil List, the inability to provide for his family was an unforgivable failure. It was perhaps the last straw to be spending his work hours daily at the Westfield train station, in a last-ditch attempt to hide his unemployment from his family.

Various accounts spoke of Helen List's overbearing manner towards John List, blaming him for their financial problems which may have added insult to injury.

At trial, John further maintained that the killings were conceived as an act of kindness, a statement belied by the extremity of execution. He also described his concerns over his 16-year-old daughter Patricia's interest in acting, and the fact that Helen, his 45-year-old wife, was not attending church.

His misplaced sense of religious duty led to the massacre uncovered by George Zhelesnik, the Westfield patrolman who responded to the neighbors' report on December 7, 1971.

"For the salvation of his family, he had to act as he did," defense attorney Elijah L. Miller Jr. insisted at List's trial. An additional defense (and List's autobiographical account of the murders) maintained that the massacre was a result of PTSD which John was suffering from, post his experiences in World War II.

That John Emil List breathed his last on a Good Friday is an unspeakable irony. The place where his house was built, indeed its entire surroundings, is unrecognizable today - houses are new or rebuilt in different designs.

Some became Tudors with leaded glass and wrought-iron door hardware. Historical markers of John List's existence have been erased from the town – only graves remain. He was a man unable to reconcile his religious beliefs with the changing values of a turbulent era.

Today, he has been pigeon-holed into a ghost story, no less than a Bogeyman like him deserves.

Chapter 6:

Writing His Own Crimes

Kicevo is a small city in the Western area of The Republic of Macedonia. It sits between two cities, Ohrid and Gostivar, and is located in the valley of the Mount Bistra, particularly in the south-eastern slope. With a population of 56,000, it is safe to say that Kicevo is a fairly manageable town.

People felt safe and confident that the security in their area was airtight. However, all that changed when three elderly woman were murdered brutally. For the first time in history, the town of Kicevo had a serial killer on the loose. This became the beef of every television news show, radio program, and of course, newspapers.

People held their breath; they patiently waited for news that would bring more clues and details to the murder, but most importantly, they waited for the serial killer to be captured.

Not too far away...

Not too far away from the commotion about the city's first serial killer, 55 year old Vlado Taneski lived. Even though he was already close to retirement, Vlado was still struggling for a living: he worked as a crime journalist for two Skopje-based newspapers, *Nova Makedonija* and *Utrinski Vesnik*, but because there were no newsworthy things coming his way, money became an issue.

The rule was simple for Vlado-- no news meant no money.

So when the serial killer in Kicevo surfaced, Vlado became the "man of the hour". As a crime journalist, it was his job to find as many details as he could about the murders and bring it to his editors. The newspapers he worked for depended on him, and to their relief, Vlado didn't disappoint.

His inside knowledge about the killings of three elderly people was so extensive that the readers couldn't help but gravitate towards his column. Because of this, his editors made it a point to give emphasis to his news reports. He knew a lot of things about the killings, that other crime journalists were left scratching their heads, confused as to where he got all the juicy information and why they couldn't get their hands on the source.

On the other side, the police force were also confused.

How come one man knew about the things they didn't release in the media? More importantly, how come one man seemed to know more than they did?

The Killer and His Victims

Over three years, three elderly women were killed. Their ages ranged from 56 to 65 years old. 64 year old Mitra Simjanoska was killed in 2005, after her, Ljubica Licoska (56) died in 2007, and a year after that 65 year old Zibana Temelkoska followed.

All of them were beaten, raped, and butchered. Interestingly, all of them came from poor families, lacked education, and worked as cleaners. After they died, the serial killer wrapped their bodies in plastic bags and dumped them in random places.

Aside from them, one woman also went missing in the year 2003, but her body was never recovered.

Amidst all this, Vlado's reports raised the authorities' eyebrows (despite the fact that readers hungered for them). For one, the descriptions of the crime scene were so detailed, as if he was given the "play by play" of the event. His coverage also included things that were not released to the public, including the use of phone cord to tie and strangle the victims. When the police completed their criminal profile, only 10 out of the 8,000 men in Kicevo became "persons of interest"-- one of the ten was Vlado Taneski.

As a crime journalist, Vlado interviewed the families of the victims, he was even in court when 4 men were wrongly accused of killing Zivana Temelkoska, and in one of his reports he even said: *"What kind of creature could so such an act?"* Nothing was wrong with all these, after all, it was his job and giving little comments came with it, but it was certainly disturbing he was one of the suspects.

When the police released a statement on June 22, 2008, saying that they had captured the killer, Vlado didn't waste time-- he went straight to the police station to get the beef out of this new progress.

However, the moment he set foot in the precinct, he was arrested; apparently, his DNA matched the sperm found at the crime scene. The police were ecstatic: they had a lot of questions to ask and since the killer himself was there, they would be able to do so now.

The thing was, Vlado Taneski killed himself the very next day; reports said he was drowned in a bucket of water, but the public were suspicious about the real cause of death. Sure, they instantly accepted the fact that he was the killer, but they couldn't get their minds to accept that a man took his own life by drowning in a bucket of water.

Why did he do it?

Aside from the obvious reason that he would have more money if he had interesting crime news to write, people didn't immediately see any motive for Vlado to murder anyone. For one, he was described as a "mild-mannered" and "well-educated" individual. He had two children and a seemingly satisfying marriage.

But deep inside, Vlado was a dark man.

He kept a separate vacation house where various pornographic videos were stored. Vlado also appeared to have hated his mother, whom he had a very bad relationship with. According to stories, after his father killed himself in 1990, the bad relationship turned worse.

It seemed like the darkness which prompted him to kill was rooted in the woman who had given birth to him: all his victims were near his mother's age, and as cleaners, they had the same occupation as hers. Worse, all of them even knew his mother personally. Profilers believed it was a very strong symbolism.

Below is an example of what he had written in one of his reports about the serial killings:

"The reason behind the killing is still unclear. Both women were acquaintances and even lived in the same town. Currently, the authorities are investigating few suspects who could be connected to the cases, which appears to be the workings of a serial killer."

And the exact sentence which brought suspicion:

"The latest body was found in a rubbish dump. It had been *tied with a piece of phone cable with which the woman had been previously strangled.*"

Chapter 7 :

Gilles and The Children in His Castles

"Gilles de Rais"

Gilles de Rais was "probably" born in 1405 to parents,

Marie de Craon and Guy II de Montmorency-Laval. Not much is known about his childhood but according to stories, he was a highly intelligent child: aside from his fluency in Latin, he also advanced in military studies, and intellectual and moral development.

After his parents died in 1415, Gilles and Rene de la Suze, his brother, were transferred to the care of their maternal grandfather, Jean de Craon. Jean was a "scheming" man-- he wanted fortune and he thought he could get it by pairing young Gilles to various rich women. In 1420, he succeeded: 15 year old Gilles married Catherine de Thouars, an heiress from Brittany. Marie, their only child, was born in 1429.

Knowing his extensive knowledge in military strategies, the positive highlight of Gilles' life was undoubtedly his rise as a strategist. Once, when Duke John VI of Montfort was captured, 16 year old Gilles was able to strategize his release. Because of this, he was awarded with land grants which he converted into money.

For 8 years (from the year 1427 to 1435), Gilles became a commander in the Royal Army; he was well known for his reckless activities, especially during wars. In 1429, the year his daughter was born, Gilles was with Joan of Arc-- they were arranging some campaigns concerning English foes and Bulgarian allies.

In his years, Gilles was described as reckless not just in military fights, but also in the use of money. In fact, when his grandfather died in 1432, he left his sword and breastplate to Rene (Gilles' younger brother), as a symbol of displeasure for the way Gilles was spending the carefully acquired fortune.

From Riches to Rags

You might ask where he could possibly have spent all his fortune when his military career didn't need much in the way of finance (as it was provided for by the government)... well, it was spent on his life goals, which included a lot of things like building the Chapel of Holy Innocents and creating a theatrical play called "Le Mistere du Siege d'Orleans".

Once the chapel was completed, Gilles wore a self-designed robe to officiate it. The play he created was just as extravagant: it had 20,000 lines, 140 speaking parts, and required at least 500 extras. When the play was under production, Gilles was already at the verge of bankruptcy: he had previously sold most of his properties, except for those owned solely by his wife and except for two other castles located in Ingrandes and Anjou, Champtoce-sur-Loire.

His desire to complete the play was so great that half of the sales money was used to finance the spectacle. To say that the play was luxurious was an understatement; the truth is it was very wasteful. For instance, 600 costumes were made for it, but all of them were only used once-- they were disposed right after and were replaced with another set of costumes for the next show.

His actions were already deplorable, but wait until you hear that this former military man had killed at least 80 children, in the span of just one year.

Hatred for Children

Gilles confessed to his own crimes: he said that he killed children from the spring of 1432 to the spring of 1433. The first set of killings happened in Champtoce-sur-Loire, an area in western France where he had a mansion.

Then, when he moved to another area in western France (particularly in Machecoul), he was reported to have killed "a great but uncertain number of children" after he had sodomized them. Please note that according to some accounts he didn't always kill them himself-- at times, he ordered some of his men to do the killings.

While there was no evidence of the murders that happened in Champtoce-sur-Loire, there was a *documented* confession of what he did in Machecoul; more over, in 1437, at least 40 bodies of children were discovered in the area.

It all started with Jeudon (not his first name), a young boy of only 12 who was "snatched". The child's disappearance resulted in a commotion because Jeudon was the apprentice of Guillaume Hilairet. According to stories, 2 of Gilles' cousins approached Guillaume because they wanted to "borrow" the boy in the pretense that Jeudon would only send a message to Machecoul.

After a few days, the child still hadn't returned, so Guillaume questioned the two noblemen, but they insisted that they knew not where Jeudon was; they could only assume that the 12 year old was abducted by thieves or was made into a page. Their "innocence," however, was belied by Guillaume, Catherine (Gilles' wife), Jeudon's father, and 5 others from Machecoul.

In a biography of Gilles written by Jean Benedetti, Jean told the story of how the children were killed: the tale goes that young children would be treated extremely well-- they were provided with expensive clothes and sent to eat sumptuous meals, including hippocras, a drink made of wine mixed with sugar and spices, which also acted as stimulant.

After making the boy at ease he would then be brought to the upper room where Gilles and "his immediate circle" would be waiting. The child's shock about his real situation would then be Gilles' source of extreme pleasure.

To prevent the child from crying out, Gilles would use a rope and hung him on a hook. Poitu, Gilles' body servant, said that once hanged, the master would masturbate on the child's belly or on his thigh. After the sexual harassment, the child would be taken down and Gilles would "placate" him with comforting words, telling him that he wouldn't be hurt and that he was only going to play with him.

It was a lie, of course, because as soon as the words were spoken, Gilles, his cousins, Pouti, or his other servants, would kill the child. The methods varied: sometimes, they were decapitated, at times, their neck was broken. When Gilles was in the mood, the victims would be tortured, dismembered, or slashed at the throat.

The crime was such a routine that the perpetrators even kept a double-edged sword at hand-- ready to be used anytime the urge to murder someone arose. The monster, unfortunately, knew no bounds when it came to his sexual gratification: there were instances when the child was already dead before he would be aroused. When there were no boys to kill, Gilles would look for young girls.

Gilles de Rais didn't deny these things, if any, he seemed proud to have performed his crimes. In one of his confessions, he even added that after the victim's death, he would pick the ones with "the most handsome face and limbs" and would hold them up to be admired.

He would kiss them, and cut them open because he "took delight at the sight of their inner organs". Gilles also did these abhorrent things even when the child was *still* breathing-- in those instances, he would sit beside them *while* they died and he would laugh at their pain.

Once the hunger for sexual pleasure had been fed, the victims would then be burnt, not by Gilles but by Poitu and another servant named Henriet. These "disposals" happened right inside Gilles' room, by the fireplace. They would burn the clothes piece by piece so that it would incinerate slowly and the smell would be lessened.

The ashes of the victims never reached their grieving families-- they were scattered in several hiding places including a cesspit and a moat.

Trial and Death by Fire and Rope

On May 15, 1440, a dispute at the church of Saint Ettiene

de Mer Morte forced Gilles to kidnap one of the clerics. This action resulted in an immediate investigation (as commanded by the Bishop of Nantes) which revealed the evidences of his serial killings. It was an accidental discovery to say the least and the evidences were never named, but it didn't stop the government and the church from arresting him on September of the same year.

Even Duke John VI, the Duke of Brittany who was an avid protector of Gilles, turned his back on him because of the "heaviness" of the crimes, which included not just murder, but also sodomy and heresy.

It also didn't help Gilles when Poitu and Henriet (his servants), Catherine (his wife), and other witnesses, took a stand against him. On October 21 of the same year, the former military man-turned-serial killer confessed to his crimes-- his confessions were so graphic that the judges asked the worst of it to be "stricken from the record". When the news of the crimes spread, many parents testified that their children also went to Gilles' castle to beg for food, but they never returned.

Due to these numerous accusations, and the fact that most victims were burnt, the authorities couldn't give the exact number of deaths caused by Gilles: the estimation is 140, the range was from 80 to 200, but some reports even mentioned a number as high as 600. Although the victims were predominantly boys, some girls were included in the count.

After their testimonies, Poitu, Henriet, and Gilles were deemed guilty by the court -- all of them were sentenced to die on October 26. At 9:00 am of that day, the three were hanged and burnt; reports said Gilles' body was cut down before it was consumed by flames. Gilles wish to be buried in the church of the monastery of the Notre Dam des Carmes in Nantes, was granted.

It was a very fitting end because Gilles also hanged his victims, and he also burnt them after death.

Chapter 8:

Killing Therapy

"Portofino harbor right" by Stan Shebs. Licensed under CC BY-SA 3.0 via Commons - https://commons.wikimedia.org/wiki/File:Portofino_h arbor_right.jpg#/media/File:Portofino_harbor_right.jp g

In just 7 months, from October of 1997 to May 1998, 17 people were killed in Italian Riviera-- 9 women and 8 men-- all died under the hands of Donato "Walter" Bilancia. As of now, he is imprisoned and will probably have no chance of freedom, but before we go into details about his incarceration, let's first discuss the crimes he did, and why he did them.

Potential Serial Killer

Many criminal profilers of today would agree on the concept of Macdonald Triad or the triad of sociopathy. This triad composes of fire setting (love to burn things), enuresis (frequent bedwetting), and cruelty to animals. According to the concept, if one child has all these three behavioral characteristics (or even just a combination of two), then he will probably have some tendency to become violent in the future.

But profilers also agree that some violent men are unpredictable, like Donato Bilancia. He didn't have three of the Macdonald Triad, he didn't even have two, he only had one, and yet, he became one of the world's scariest serial killers.

Donato was born in 1951, in Potenza in Southern Italy. He was just 5 years old when his family moved to Northern Italy, first to Piedmont, then to Genoa. His family appeared to be somewhat dysfunctional, that, or they had a bad sense of humor.

Apparently, Donato was a bedwetter from when he was young up to the age of 10 or 12. No one in the house helped him conquer it; they even used it as an ammunition against him. His mother shamed him by drying his bedsheets on the balcony, where all their neighbors could see it while his aunt reached the point of abusing him by pulling his pants down in front of his cousins for them to see his underdeveloped penis.

No clear reasons were given, but at the age of 14, Donato started calling himself "Walter", he also dropped out of school and began working odd jobs like being a mechanic, a bartender, and a delivery boy.

Early Crime Potential

He was still a minor when Walter stole a motor scooter; on another occasion, he stole a truck filled with Christmas sweets. In the year 1974, he acquired a gun illegally and was jailed for it.

One of his robbery escapades sent him to prison for 18 months, but ironically speaking, he wasn't apprehended for any form of violence until he was 47 years old. Once, he was also admitted to Genoa General Hospital (psychiatric division), but he escaped.

Serial Killer

Many reports mentioned that Walter was a "compulsive gambler". This was further made worse by the fact that he lived alone, which meant no one was there to "tame" his instincts to gamble. His first murder was actually related to a "rigged card game" which was presented to him by a friend.

Because he believed that he was intentionally lured into that game (where he lost $267,000), he killed that friend by strangling him. Walter was not caught because the police thought that the cause of death was simply heart attack. Still feeling the need for vengeance for his loss, Walter killed the game operator next, and then he murdered the game operator's wife. Both of them were shot.

After three victims, Walter had the taste of murder and he liked it. In his mind, he knew that it was only a matter of time before he craved for another life, due to this, he made it a point to carry a loaded .38 revolver wherever he went.

In the same month, he followed a jeweler home to rob his shop and kill him in the process. He didn't plan on killing anyone else, but because the jeweler's wife witnessed the whole thing and wouldn't stop screaming, he didn't hesitate to shoot her, too. Only then did he empty the safe where the jewels were. After them, a money changer became the next victim (he also robbed him after the murder).

2 months later, he murdered a night watchman who was only doing his job rounding the neighborhood. Later on, Walter would confess that he did the crime simply because he hated night watchmen.

Two prostitutes became his next victims, one was Albanian, and the other was Russian. A second money changer died in his hands and his safe, too, was emptied.

In March of 1998, he forced a prostitute to perform fellatio on him, when she disagreed, he took his gun and made her do it at gunpoint. Two night watchmen noticed the commotion and attempted to interrupt, but Walter would have none of their intrusion, so he immediately shot them. The prostitute, too, was shot, but she survived, and it was her description which helped the police develop a sketch of Walter (she would also testify against him later).

Two prostitutes were killed after that, one was Ukrainian and the other was Nigerian and one other prostitute was robbed, but she wasn't killed.

At this point, Walter was already unstoppable; his urge to

kill was growing by the minute and he couldn't stay still. On April 12, 1998, he boarded a train going to Venice because he "wanted to kill a woman". He didn't have anything else in mind, he just desired to use his pistol, point it on a womanly head, fire it, and see the victim go limp and lifeless.

He searched for and spotted a woman traveling alone; he followed her to the restroom and locked the room with a skeleton key. Walter didn't wait-- he took his gun and shot her dead. He also took her train ticket and traveled as if he had done nothing wrong.

Less than a week later, he boarded a train to San Remo and did the same thing: followed a woman to the toilet, locked the door, and shot her dead. To minimize the noise created by the shot, he used his jacket as the silencer. When Walter noticed that the woman was wearing black underwear, he got excited, so he masturbated on the corpse and used her clothes to clean up.

Because the women murdered on the train stations were not prostitutes, but were well-liked, and respected personalities, the public was outraged and a police task force was created to find the killer.

The last kill had been a gasoline store attendant, and as with his other cases, Walter also robbed the store.

Arrest

One of the prostitutes remembered the Black Mercedes car, and based from that input, the police considered Walter as "suspect number 1". They tailed him for ten days and collected DNA samples from the cups he used and the cigarette butts he disposed.

Not before long, the police determined that his DNA matched the one at the crime scenes. On May of 1998, he was arrested at his home on Genova, Italy and within two days, he confessed to his crimes.

Analysis

According to *Health Psychology Consultacy*, Walter's violence was rooted in his difficult formative years. The article mentioned that young Walter was beaten by his father and it made the boy believe that he did something wrong or that there was something wrong with him. The fear, anxiety, and low self-esteem manifested through frequent bedwetting, the insults of his mother and his aunt also made things rougher for him.

His victims were mostly women and this was probably because of the shaming he got from them-- from his mother, aunt, and the prostitutes who belittled him because of his penis size. Because he hated himself, he decided to change his name-- a symbolism of throwing away the old him.

If you'll notice, his petty crimes started right after he changed his name; this was probably due to his need to prove his "manliness". In his mind, the more petty crimes he committed, the manlier he got. Only, these little crimes progressed into something more sinister.

Despite being a loner, Walter still needed friends-- a source of companionship and caring; that was why he took it badly when a man he considered his friend betrayed him. It was the last straw.

When he killed his friend, it felt good, so he craved to do it again. In other words, killing became Walter's therapy. And because it was a therapy, he didn't need a strategy; he didn't need to think things through. That was why he had no definite MO, his crimes were messy, and he never tried to hide the body after the crime.

For Walter, the main goal was to kill because it felt good-- he didn't need a style to do it.

Conclusion

Thank you again for purchasing this book!

Drugs, family problems, repressed sexuality, financial constraints, narcissistic tendencies, and hunger for power - all these could cause a person to deviate from the righteous path. Some would be able to find their way back, but others would be in too deep to be rescued.

The safety of the community not only rests in the hands of the law, but also on the residents who choose to be more aware of their surroundings and brave enough to report anything suspicious. In other words, it's a cooperation, if one neglects his or her duty, lives could be at stake.

If you enjoyed this book would you be kind enough to leave us a review on Amazon? It is very much appreciated, thank you so much!

I hope you enjoyed this book, thank you and good luck!

Check Out My Other Books

Below you'll find some of my other popular books that are popular on Amazon and Kindle as well. You can visit my author page on Amazon to see other work done by me. (Brody Clayton).

True Murder Stories

Women Who Kill

Serial Killers

Cold Cases True Crime

Serial Killers – Volume 2

Cold Cases True Crime – Volume 2

True Crime

True Crime – Volume 2

True Crime – Volume 3

Serial Killers True Crime

Serial Killers True Crime – Volume 2

Serial Killers True Crime – Volume 3

Serial Killers True Crime – Volume 4

True Crime Stories

You can simply search for these titles on the Amazon website with my name to find them.

LIBRARY BUGS
BOOKS

Like FREE books?

Would you like them delivered to you every week?

Do you like non-fiction books on a huge range of different topics?

We send out FREE e-books every week so we can share our books with the world!

We have FREE books every week on AMAZON that we send to our email list. If you want in, then visit the link below to sign up and sit back and wait for new books to be sent straight to your inbox!

It couldn't be simpler!

www.LibraryBugs.com

If you want FREE books delivered straight to your inbox, then visit the link above and soon you'll be receiving a great list of FREE e-books every week!

Enjoy :)

Links to Pictures

Dean Corll -
https://en.wikipedia.org/wiki/Dean_Corll#/media/File:
Dean_Corll.jpg

Jim Jones -
https://en.wikipedia.org/wiki/Jim_Jones#/media/File:0
2-jones-jim_ji.jpg

Leo Ryan -
https://en.wikipedia.org/wiki/Jim_Jones#/media/File:1
973_Congressional_Pictorial_Leo_Ryan.jpg

Jonestown -
https://en.wikipedia.org/wiki/Jonestown#/media/File:J
onestown_Memorial_Service_Pictures.jpg

Gilles de Rais -
https://en.wikipedia.org/wiki/Gilles_de_Rais#/media/Fi
le:Gillesderais1835.jpg

Printed in Great Britain
by Amazon